The
Bourton-on-t
Walkabout.

GW00538084

Bourton on the Water in the 1960's

Reardon

A Cotswold Village Trail
by
Peter Reardon

Published by
REARDON PUBLISHING
56, Upper Norwood Street, Leckhampton,
Cheltenham, Glos, GL53 0DU, England, E.U.
tel: 01242 231800
www.reardon.co.uk

Reardon Publishing
Copyright © 2000

Written and Researched
by
Peter Reardon

ISBN 1 873877 43 9

Drawings and Maps
by
Peter Reardon

Layout & Design
by
Nicholas Reardon

Cover Photo is of Mill Bridge
by
David Morris
Bourton on the Water

Printed by
Stoate and Bishop Ltd
Cheltenham

A Gem in the Cotswolds

The Old Fosse Way bridge over the River Windrush at the Entrance to Bourton on the Water

The Cotswolds is an area of really outstanding natural beauty. With its rolling hills, wide open views, cosy valleys, rivers and streams and its enchanting little towns and villages there is nowhere else in the country quite like it. One of these charming little villages is Bourton on the Water.

To many motorists today, Bourton on the Water is just words on a road sign. But for the visitor to the Cotswolds, Bourton is a little Gem, having a lot to offer in many ways depending on one's interests.

Bourton straddles the River Windrush which flows quietly through the village from north of Toddington to join the River Thames at Newbridge. near Oxford. It is very pleasant to sit on the Green on a fine day and watch the wildlife - ducks, moorhens, etc - on and around the river. The children love watching them swimming around.

It is hoped that your visit to the Cotswolds and specially to Bourton on the Water was most enjoyable, then maybe those memories will draw you to making another call in the future.

Peter T. Reardon.

The Walks.

There are three walks here and all three start and finish in the **High Street**, which makes things easier for everyone as they can also be linked together to make one long walk. The Start Point is outside the Model Railway Exhibition premises on the High Street near a signpost pointing to the various village attractions just about opposite the footbridge over the River Windrush, this is also where the Guide Friday vintage open air bus collects visitors for scenic tours.

No:1   Church and Bridges   (30 Min Walk . . . .).

Start by walking NW (Turn Right) along the High Street towards the Lansdown area passing the War Memorial on your left. On arriving at the Cross roads go straight on over. Soon you will pass toilets on your right on the corner of Rectory Lane, a little way on you will pass the entrance to the Church of St Lawrence.

The Church of St. Lawrence is well worth a visit and a chance to enjoy a few moments of peace and tranquillity in this busy world of ours, the Church welcomes visitors but please remember that this is a house of God so please respect Church Services and the need to close at times.

St Lawrences Church tower complete with dome and urns

The Skull and Crossbones over the West door of the Church of St Lawrence

Continue on passing School Lane then a garage on your right and a bit further along you will come to the Mouse Trap Inn. Cross the road here but be careful as it is a fairly busy road. Once across continue in the same direction (heading out of the Village) keeping a lookout for a Public Footpath Sign for the Windrush Way next to the Strathspey Guest House.

Follow the Footpath Sign pointing left along a pathway lined with trees to the river (not the first turning on the Left), then go left alongside the River Windrush, then right over a bridge crossing the river and then left alongside the river first following a  *A Minnow seen in the River* hedge then fence to your right with river to your left to a kissing gate in a fence.

Cotswold Sheep

Once through the gate bear right and head for the corner of the field between a wall and a fence at the back of the houses. There you will see another kissing gate. Go through and along a narrow alley to join Sherbourne Street. Turn left and go along, passing the Duke of Wellington Inn, till you come to the

Mill Bridge over the River Windrush, the Motor Museum on your left, the War Memorial on your right and a cross roads. Here turn right and head up the High Street to the Model Railway Exhibition. The picture on the left shows the view as you enter Sherbourne Street and below is the wonderful view of the old mill now the Motor Museum as seen from over the River Windrush.

A Quiet spot in Bourton on the Water

Mill Bridge by the Old Mill

End of Walk 1.

Cotswold Motoring Museum

The Cotswold Motoring Museum is a unique collection of cars, motorcycles and caravans. The Museum also contains lots of exciting memorabilia, including teddy bears, aeroplanes and a rare collection of pedal cars. Opened in 1978 the Museum housed the personal collection of just one man, and includes one of the largest collections of metal motoring signs.

The most famous inhabitant of the museum is Brum, the yellow toy car from the BBC children's series.
Children come from everywhere to visit him.

The Cotswold Motoring Museum offers all visitors, young and old, an experience to remember.

The Museum is open from March to October 10am - 6pm.

Admission   Adults   £2.25   Cotswold Motoring Museum
           Children £1.25   & Toy Collection
           Family   £6.50   Bourton-on-the-Water
Concessions for members   Gloucestershire
of **csma**   tel: 01451 821255

COUNTRY CRAFTS

The largest selection of gifts in
Bourton on the Water
Stockists of Walkers Shortbread,
Cotswold Cider, Mead, Honey,
Broadland Wine, Belgium Chocolates.

-: *Gift Wrapping Service* :-

Leonardo Gifts, Florence, Elisa,
Crabtree & Evelyn, Heredities,
Kaiser Porcelain, Robert Harrop,
Bowbrook Studios, Tiptree,
Cathness Glass, Christmas Hampers.
4 The Chestnuts, Bourton on the Water,
GL54 2AN 01451 820102

Maps - Guide Books - Walking Books -
Stamps - Postcards

**Where to go and What
to see in the Cotswolds**

For information on places to visit,
events and transport information,

visit

BOURTON-ON-THE-WATER
VISITOR INFORMATION
CENTRE

Victoria Street, Bourton-on-the-Water
GL54 2BU
Tel; 01451 820211   Fax; 01451 821103

Where to stay? Use our
Accommodation Booking Service

No:2   Bridges and Birds   (45 Min Walk + + + +).

High Bridge, the first bridge of the walk

Our second walk is named Bridges and Birds and you will soon see the reason for this as Bourton on the Water is also known as the Venice of the Cotswolds and with this walk you will see lots of Bridges and as for the Birds well you will walk very near one of Bourtons famous attractions "Birdland".

Start off by crossing the road and on to a footbridge over the River Windrush, this bridge pictured above is called High Bridge and has a Tourist Information Sign on it. Once over the bridge turn left and walk beside the river passing the famous Victoria Hall on your right. Follow the river till you come to two bridges side by side, the first one is called New Bridge by the Kingsbridge Inn (buy a drink and ask at the Inn why they are not called the Newbridge Inn). Cross the road also passing another small bridge and this one is called Payne's Bridge and now go along the path with the river still to your left.

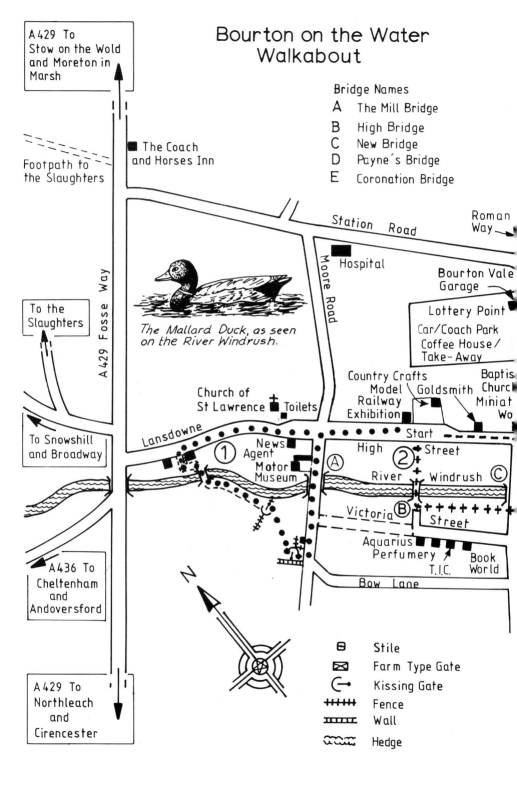

Bourton on the Water Walkabout

A429 To
Stow on the Wold
and Moreton in
Marsh

Footpath to
the Slaughters

The Coach
and Horses Inn

Bridge Names

A The Mill Bridge
B High Bridge
C New Bridge
D Payne's Bridge
E Coronation Bridge

Station Road

Roman Way

A429 Fosse Way

To the
Slaughters

Moore Road

Hospital

Bourton Vale
Garage

Lottery Point
Car/Coach Park
Coffee House/
Take-Away

The Mallard Duck, as seen
on the River Windrush.

Country Crafts
Model
Railway
Exhibition

Goldsmith

Baptis
Churc
Miniat
Wo

Church of
St Lawrence

Toilets

Lansdowne

Start

To Snowshill
and Broadway

News
Agent
Motor
Museum

High

Street

River

Windrush

(1)

(A)

(2)

(B)

(C)

Victoria

Street

A436 To
Cheltenham
and
Andoversford

N

Aquarius
Perfumery
T.I.C.

Book
World

Bow Lane

A429 To
Northleach
and
Cirencester

Stile

Farm Type Gate

Kissing Gate

Fence

Wall

Hedge

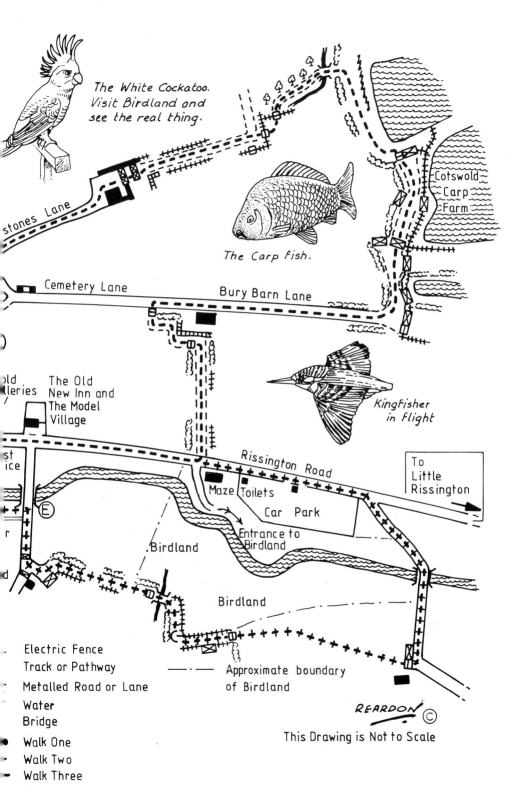

The White Cockatoo.
Visit Birdland and
see the real thing.

stones Lane

The Carp fish.

Cotswold
Carp
Farm

Cemetery Lane   Bury Barn Lane

Kingfisher
in flight

old
leries

The Old
New Inn and
The Model
Village

st
ice

Rissington Road

To
Little
Rissington

E

Maze Toilets

Car Park

Entrance to
Birdland

.Birdland

Birdland

Electric Fence
Track or Pathway   — · — Approximate boundary
Metalled Road or Lane   of Birdland
Water
Bridge

Walk One

Walk Two

Walk Three

REARDON ©

This Drawing is Not to Scale

New Bridge by the Kingsbridge Inn

A small bridge called Payne's Bridge

On your right for a short distance are some attractive little shops followed by private houses. At the end of the path you come to another bridge with E.R. on it and this bridge is called Coronation Bridge and is just by a

Moorhen

ford, (a river crossing and not the make of car !) now turn right and follow the lane to a gate.

Coronation Bridge

(At this point if you get a little confused see the central map, you will infact be going on public footpaths so keep a look out for green signs and yellow disks). Go through the gate. Ignore the gate ahead

The Water Vole

and bear left towards another gate. Again, ignore this gate and go left of it along a path between a hedge and fence.

Along this path you will come to the boundary line of Birdland on your left. A little further along the path you will come to a stile. Go over this and cross the little footbridge over a stream. Go right between fence on the left and hedge on the right and you will arrive at a kissing gate. Pass through and follow the path

The Emperor Dragonfly

with the Birdland boundary fence to your left, (warning please keep children under supervision at this point and do not touch the fence) and passing a gate in the fence on your right you will come to a stile. Go over the stile and follow the track in the field for about 100 yards, then bear slightly right and head along the lane after a short distance you will come to a gate and a stile. Go over the stile and bear left along the minor road / lane. Soon you will come to a bridge over the River Windrush where, after crossing it you take the left hand route.

Entrance to the Model Village at the Old New Inn

This will bring you to the Rissington Road where you turn left and head back into Bourton, passing the attractions of the Dragonfly Maze, Birdland and Model Village. If you want to cross the road it is advisable to wait till after the right hand bend opposite the Post Office as traffic is less and slower.

End of Walk 2

The Old New Inn & Model Village

The Old New Inn is a Traditional Country Inn where you can enjoy a drink and chat in front of real log fires. The Model Village at the rear of the Inn is a 1/9th replica in local stone of the village of Bourton on the Water

E-mail: old_new_inn@compuserve.com
Telephone: 01451 820467 Fax: 01451 810236

No:3 Lakes and Wildlife (60 Min Walk - - - -).

From the Model Railway Exhibition premises go left in a SE direction past the shops on the opposite side to the river and just  past the Gold Smiths you come to the junction of Station Road and Rissington Road. Go left along Station Road passing the Baptist Church on your left and a big car park and petrol station, again on your left. Go past the petrol station for a short distance and take the first right (if you reach Roman Way you have missed it !), before Station Road bears left, is a small road called Cemetery Lane. Take this

Meadow Buttercup

road and after a few yards it is joined by Greystones Lane. Go left along this lane and soon you will arrive at a Farm. Here bear left and then right round the house and head for two pairs of farm gates. On your left you will have a row of buildings and a yard on the right. Go through the right hand gate of the first pair, then the right hand gate of the second pair and on to a track heading straight ahead. Shut the

The Brown Hare

gates and make sure they are properly secure. The track goes between fences on either side until it looks like a dead end. The track bears left but you come to two stiles in the fence, one straight ahead, the other on the right. Go straight ahead over the stile and immediately on your left in a fence is another stile. Go over this stile, turn right, and you will be on a short path between trees on your left and a little stream on your right.

The Stoate

After a short walk along this path you will come to a little bridge over the stream. Cross the bridge, through the gap in the hedge and turn right. You now have a hedge on your right and an electric fence on your left with a lake the other side of the fence. Take

SYCAMORE LEAF
AND SEED

advantage of the peace and quiet as you walk along by the lake, except perhaps for the sound of ducks and moorhens on the lake. After a while you will come to a gate and stile. Go over the stile and head on down a track between a hedge on the right and hedge/fence on the left, passing another lake on your left. About halfway along this track you will pass two gates, one left, one right, but ignore both of them and keep going. Continue on along the track till you come to another gate. Go through this gate, ignoring another one on the right and carry on passing another on your left till you reach the end of the track with two gates and a stile on the left. Here you go right along Bury Barn Lane. You will come to a big house on the left surrounded by trees and a few paces on you will see a stile in the

FROG

hedge with a path going downhill through the trees. Go over this stile and follow the path till you come to another stile. Over again, bear right and follow this path between the hedge on your right and fence on your left till you come to the main Rissington Road. Here, turn right and follow the road back in to Bourton on the Water where you can finish up with refreshments and then go back to your car.

End of Walk 3

This now ends our set of walks around this lovely Cotswold village of Bourton on the Water and we do hope that you have enjoyed yourselves, now that you know your way around we suggest that you take time and explore for there is so much to see and do.

A Moorhen

Wold Galleries
Halford House, Station Road,
Bourton-on-the-Water GL54 2AA
Tel: 01451 822092

Open every day except Tuesday
10am - 5pm

For over thirty years Wold Galleries have featured the finest oils, watercolours, pastels and prints by a number of artists who are well known regionally and nationally for their work. The display also includes a varied selection of ceramics, glass and sculpture.

A regular programme of exhibitions ensures that there is always a good reason to call in!